Rain and Hail

by Cara Torrance

OXFORD
UNIVERSITY PRESS
AUSTRALIA & NEW ZEALAND

The rain hits down on the roof.

It is a wet week.

In the rain you can feel a chill. You need a coat.

You need to get the pets in.
They are all wet.

You hear the dog bark. Her ears and her tail are down.

You can pat her.
Now she feels good.

In the rain you might see lights.

You might hear a boom in the air.

Now you see hail.
Secure the door and go in.

The power might go down.
You can get a torch.

You can get this oil light, too.

This is a wood burner.
You can cook on it.

You can get a pot to boil.
The liquid will be hot.

You can get a cool sip, too.

pure

Rain and hail can be fun!